# Like a Mighty Rushing Wind

Bill Vincent

Published by RWG Publishing, 2021.

While every precaution has been taken in the preparation of this book, the publisher assumes no responsibility for errors or omissions, or for damages resulting from the use of the information contained herein.

LIKE A MIGHTY RUSHING WIND

**First edition. August 16, 2021.**

Copyright © 2021 Bill Vincent.

Written by Bill Vincent.

# Also by Bill Vincent

Building a Prototype Church: Divine Strategies Released
Experience God's Love: By Revival Waves of Glory School of the Supernatural
Glory: Expanding God's Presence
Glory: Increasing God's Presence
Glory: Kingdom Presence of God
Glory: Pursuing God's Presence
Glory: Revival Presence of God
Rapture Revelations: Jesus Is Coming
The Prototype Church: Heaven's Strategies for Today's Church
The Secret Place of God's Power
Transitioning Into a Prototype Church: New Church Arising
Spiritual Warfare Made Simple
Aligning With God's Promises
A Closer Relationship With God
Armed for Battle: Spiritual Warfare Battle Commands
Breakthrough of Spiritual Strongholds
Desperate for God's Presence: Understanding Supernatural Atmospheres
Destroying the Jezebel Spirit: How to Overcome the Spirit Before It Destroys You!
Discerning Your Call of God
Glory: Expanding God's Presence: Discover How to Manifest God's Glory

Glory: Kingdom Presence Of God: Secrets to Becoming Ambassadors of Christ
Satan's Open Doors: Access Denied
Spiritual Warfare: The Complete Collection
The War for Spiritual Battles: Identify Satan's Strategies
Understanding Heaven's Court System: Explosive Life Changing Secrets
A Godly Shaking: Don't Create Waves
Faith: A Connection of God's Power
Global Warning: Prophetic Details Revealed
Overcoming Obstacles
Spiritual Leadership: Kingdom Foundation Principles
Glory: Revival Presence of God: Discover How to Release Revival Glory
Increasing Your Prophetic Gift: Developing a Pure Prophetic Flow
Millions of Churches: Why Is the World Going to Hell?
The Supernatural Realm: Discover Heaven's Secrets
The Unsearchable Riches of Christ: Chosen to be Sons of God
Deep Hunger: God Will Change Your Appetite Toward Him
Defeating the Demonic Realm
Glory: Increasing God's Presence: Discover New Waves of God's Glory
Growing In the Prophetic: Developing a Prophetic Voice
Healing After Divorce: Grace, Mercy and Remarriage
Love is Waiting
Awakening of Miracles: Personal Testimonies of God's Healing Power
Deception and Consequences Revealed: You Shall Know the Truth and the Truth Shall Set You Free
Overcoming the Power of Lust
Cover Up and Save Yourself: Revealing Sexy is Not Sexy
Heaven's Court System: Bringing Justice for All
The Angry Fighter's Story: Harness the Fire Within
The Wrestler: The Pursuit of a Dream
Beginning the Courts of Heaven: Understanding the Basics

Breaking Curses: Legal Rights in the Courts of Heaven
Writing and Publishing a Book: Secrets of a Christian Author
How to Write a Book: Step by Step Guide
The Anointing: Fresh Oil of God's Presence
Spiritual Leadership: Kingdom Foundation Principles Second Edition
The Courts of Heaven: How to Present Your Case
The Jezebel Spirit: Tactics of Jezebel's Control
Heaven's Angels: The Nature and Ranking of Angels
Don't Know What to Do?: Discover Promotion in the Wilderness
Word of the Lord: Prophetic Word for 2020
The Coronavirus Prophecy
Increase Your Anointing: Discover the Supernatural
Apostolic Breakthrough: Birthing God's Purposes
The Healing Power of God: Releasing the Power of the Holy Spirit
The Secret Place of God's Power: Revelations of God's Word
The Rapture: Details of the Second Coming of Christ
Increase of Revelation and Restoration: Reveal, Recover & Restore
Leadership vs Management
Restoration of the Soul: The Presence of God Changes Everything
Building a Prototype Church: The Church is in a Season of Profound of Change
Keys to Receiving Your Miracle: Miracles Happen Today
The Resurrection Power of God: Great Exploits of God
Transitioning to the Prototype Church: The Church is in a Season of Profound of Transition
Waves of Revival: Expect the Unexpected
The Stronghold of Jezebel: A True Story of a Man's Journey
Glory: Pursuing God's Presence: Revealing Secrets
Like a Mighty Rushing Wind
Steps to Revival

Watch for more at https://revivalwavesofgloryministries.com/.

This book was transcribed from one of the thousands of sermons of Bill Vincent. Please realize this as you read this book. Thanks for your purchase and support.

# Like a Mighty Rushing Wind

Recently, I gave notice that God been speaking to me about end times, some depths of things and some of the things that I thought was so astounding, mind blowing that shake the very core of your being. Now, just so you know, I'm not talking about that tonight, but I am referring to some scriptures that opened me up into this level that I believe that God want to take us to. Because I believe there's more. How many know that God want us to do more even in the time that we're in right now. Me and my house last year faith is not going to work for this year. Everything is different, it's different. We're at a different level than we've ever been before, and it's not pumping ourselves up, it's not lifting ourselves up, it's not saying a little bigger. If anything, I feel like I went the other direction. Come on. But it's a different level, it's a different platform, it's a different arena than we've ever been used to before. That's where we're at. That's why it doesn't fit the way it fit last time. That's why it doesn't work the way we thought it worked last time. That's why we won't understand it till it's time to understand. I don't know why we get bent out of shape. I don't know why we get concerned. I don't know why we ever get consumed by anything. I really don't know. You know, I understand the children get consumed, but I don't know why me and my wife and Sam, Paula, you know Ryan sometimes maybe and sometimes not because, you know, he's been in this lesson less than us.

But I want to understand and Ben, you know, I don't know if he's getting concerned about anything right now, but we're in a time. Where we get so consumed and that's all the devil wants. Especially when we're going to another level, and he knows we're about to do some big damage to the kingdom of hell. Come on. And I want you to understand something. Whenever somebody says we're about to do damage on the kingdom of hell, a lot of people think that we're talking about down there. Down there is a sentence down, down there being the finished work down there where they're going to end up, the damage we're doing is on the second heaven. The damage we're doing is going to be messing up every hindrance, come on, blockage, that has been going on for decades and even hundreds of years. I'm all sure my title sometime, but right now God said this, I know I'm out of order for some people, God is saying come. Come to me, this is not the title come up here. How long have we heard that? A door standing open. Come, come on. And there's always a voice crying from heaven. I want you to come up here and we begin to go for a day, for a week, for a month. But then we come back. And we get more planted on this realm when we're supposed to be in that realm. How many know it's been a lot better when we're always up there? Come on, when we had signs and wonders every week, it was better come on when we had people getting healed, set free and deliver every week, it was better. Why? Because we were not here. We were there a lot of what we're trying to do in this time that we're in and we're not the only ones. It's all across the map because we get back in the old-time tradition. We like things, tradition. I did it last year, I did it the year before. Well, guess what this year you're not and it's just the way it works. We got to break some tradition. We're going to break some religion. Why? Because we are supposed to be heaven based.

I keep seeing in the spirit scrolls. Scrolls. Chariots of Fire and Living Creatures. Let me let me say this one more time. This is why I keep seeing in the spirit. Scrolls, Chariots of Fire, and the Living Creatures. And part of me is undone by that. You read about the living creatures, but you don't read about the living creatures. Come on, you read about the horsemen in the word of God, but you don't really read it as soon as it says there's one head going this way and another head going that way, most of the church checks out, ain't that right, as soon as we start seeing that there's two headed things being spoke in the word of God, religion checks out. One has wings, one has four legs. It's like one is like a man, it's like what the world is going on and we're getting into some detail. And we started thinking, oh, my goodness, this is madness. We skip over it. But what God's been doing with me lately, it's taking me right into the nitty gritty. And I keep seeing scrolls, Chariots of Fire and Living Creatures. And. Even Isaiah had the Seraphim Angel. A Seraphim angel in Isaiah, Chapter six, who took a call and cleaned Isaiah's lips. And set his heart ablaze and commit and for commission, I want you to think about something. We're going to let's look at that scripture because we need to get into it. Isaiah, Chapter six, we're going to look at some stuff. And at first, you're going to be like, oh, my goodness, this is going to be rough. Come on. Some of you are going to already check out as soon as we get into some of the stuff. I don't know what he's talking about, so I'm just out. But that's all right. It's OK to get lost because you've got to understand, I've written books on the presence of God. I've talked about angels in those books, and I've referred to these scriptures. But God's taken me to a new depth. Why? Because we're not supposed to ignore these any longer. It's time to experience these right here, right now, right where we're at. Every time you start getting into a rut, start falling down, start getting where you need minister to an angel is going to come. Hallelujah, and he's going to wipe your lips. Hallelujah. He's going to give you exactly what you need. Hallelujah. If you need to smoke you, you're going to get your smoke. Come on.

So, verse one through seven. Come on. It was in the year of King Uzziah, and he died. That's also the Lord setting upon the throne high and lifted up and his train filled the temple. Come on. We sing a song with this, above it stood the servants. Each one had six wings. Listen to some of this detail with Twain he covered his face. Come on. He has six wings, covered his face with a couple of them and with Twain he covered his feet. So, a couple was covering his feet. And with Twain he did fly. So, you got to come on. You got to you got to think about this. He's covering his legs, his feet, and his flying. Come on, come on, this is a seraphim, covered his legs, his feet, and he's flying, I mean, his legs, his feet. What I mean, in his eyes and he is flying. I want to I want to tear down some of this just for a moment. I'm not going to tear it all down because we can't we'll never get out of here. We'll be here tomorrow morning, 5:00 a.m. still breathing heavy and going somewhere. And verse three and one cried unto another and said, holy, holy, holy is the Lord of hosts, the whole earth is full of his glory and the post of the door move at the voice of him that cried, and the house was filled with smoke. Then said, I woe is me where I am and done, and I feel like where I'm at right now thinking about all this because I am a man with unclean lips and I dwell in the midst of a people of unclean lips for my eyes have seen the king, the Lord of Hosts.

Verse six, then flew one of the Seraphim into me having a live coal in his hand, which he had taken with the tongs from the altar. So, this is the burning altar. He took a fiery coal and wiped the lips. Hmm. I want you to think about something. Here we are, Isaiah is getting to experience, do you understand where I'm at? He's getting an experience. Let me tell you something, seraphim are movable objects. They're not just position, religion teaches that seraphim's is just down there. No, they do not. We're going to get into some I'm only going to cross the threshold where God says to cross and I'm not going to cross all the way where he says, don't do it yet. But then here's where God took me. Immediately after that, scripture said, go to Revelation Chapter five. I will be reading amplified. I'm going to give some my own emphasis, and this is what I mean by my own emphasis. I mean, I'm given original definitions of what the original text meant. Revelations, Chapter five, verse eight through ten. So, if you've already checked out, just hang on, because we need to plug back in. When he had taken the scroll. I told you I was seeing scroll, the four living creatures. I told you I was seeing four living creatures. And the twenty-four elders fell down before the lamb, which is who? Christ, each one of them holding a harp, a golden bowls at full of fragrant incense, which are the prayers of the Saints who are the saints, God's people. And they sang a new song saying worthy and deserving are you to take the scroll and to break it seal. What happens when you break the seal, that means something is accomplished, that means something is happening and meant there's it's time for it. There's a new thing about to start. Seals only get broke when something else is being opened up. There are several seals that have to be open before the end of the world by the way, we're not going to get into that. And you are slain or what? What that also means is sacrificed. And with your blood, you purchased people for God from every tribe and language and people and nation. You made them to be a kingdom and priests to our God, and they will reign on the earth

See God wants us to know that he hears our prayers. I want you to understand in the midst of these scriptures, you might not hear it, but I want you to know this is what God is saying. He hears our prayers, and he has not forgotten our sons and daughters. He has not forgotten us. Come on. The scrolls spoken and revelations are like instructions. Did you know that the revelations are actually instructions for us today? Come on. And most of the church is ignoring the Book of Revelations. And all of us are or are different, but none are left out. He's calling us to come up and to get our hearts right before him and I mean right before him. We have to have our hearts right. I'm not saying get your heart right before every service. I'm not saying get your heart right. Only when you get exposed. I'm not saying only get your heart right when you finally feel guilty. We need to just get our heart right. It's a coincidence I was facing certain people, maybe, see he has commissioned us to go preach the gospel, come on with greater fire and passion, with signs and wonders of miracles that will follow. Yeah, let's do that now, let's look at Ezekiel, you want to get out there, read Ezekiel. Just read Ezekiel and everything you don't understand, read it again and again, so you'll be on Ezekiel for a couple of months. Ezekiel chapter two, verse one through seven. Before I start, God says he's calling back the priest, the Levites, and the prophets to come home. You know, we're supposed to go to heaven, we're supposed to go home, and what I mean by that, we're supposed to go get some things and bring it back to Earth. We're supposed to get our head in the clouds. We're supposed to see things by the spirit and bring them back, and they're not supposed to make sense. And here's what God told me today, I didn't get it till today. Sometimes you see things and you think they're right there. Why? Because you saw him right there, there. But many times, they're not right there. They're just near and we have to we were different eyes here and there, and we got to begin to get them lined up. And the thing is, unless you're always there, you don't identify with the with the timing of things and how long things are because you see it there. You come back here and then you start saying things and it's out of context. It doesn't make sense. It does a bit. Why? Because you're in there.

But when we finally get it connected and making sense of it, see but the devil, he tries to come and disqualify the whole thing. But see, that's a lie, the devil, and we can't disqualify it. Hey, if God said it, you know, he wants you to do it. So, talking about out there, let's start with verse one. Then he said to me, son of man, stand on your feet and I will speak to you. You know, sometimes God won't speak to you and unless you stand up. Just thought I'd put that out there. Come on, he said, literally stand up to your feet and I'll speak to you. And then he spoke to me, the spirit entered me and set me on my feet, so I believe that if the spirit had entered him, he wasn't so willing to get up. I just like to spend time thinking about questions when I read. And I heard him speaking to me and he said to me, I am sending you son a man to the children of Israel, to a rebellious people all think of Jesus, to have they have rebelled against me. They and their fathers have since revolted against me to this very day. Ain't that wonderful, God sending you to a bunch of rebellious people, I'm sending you to them who are stubborn and obstinate children, you shall say to them thus said the Lord, God, as for them, whether they listen or refuse to listen, for they are a rebellious house. Yet they will know and be fully aware of the fact that there has been a prophet among them. And you, son of man, neither fear them nor fear their words though briers and thrones all around you and you said among scorpions, neither fear their words nor be dismayed by their presence for they are a rebellious house. But you shall speak my words to them, whether they will listen or refuse to listen, for they are most rebellious.

You know when people say the harvest is ripe. Everybody gets a mentality, people are going to get saved, come into church, and lift their hands up the same day. But, you know, this world is a rebellious people. Anybody who is not into things of God especially are rebellious people right now rebelling against political things, rebelling against the government, rebelling against this rebellion against that rebellion against parents. That's what the harvest is. So, we're looking for God to send us the harvest, you know, all these churches are praying for the harvest to come in and they're going to get rebellious people, stubborn people. Come on, they're going to get a bunch of people who aren't delivered, aren't set free, they just think it's a harvest. Oh, it's a wheat field. It's not going to be all fluff. They're going to come in and they're not going to have religion, they're going to have rebellion. So, religion has no place for this that's coming. It's only places like us be able to handle places all over the nation. There are many places, not that many, but many places who can handle some of this, but most cannot. Most are going to have people come in and they're not going to be able to tame them. They're not going to be they're going to try to counsel things that need to be cast out. They're going to try to flop this, they need to say, demon, you come out now. They're going to be coming in all over the place. Churches are not going to be able to handle it. See, there are people of great darkness desperately needing Jesus Christ. Here's what God said. The plow is coming. The plow is coming. I said lord what is the plow. He said it's p period l period o period w period. I don't like to use these things unless God said to use them. Everybody uses them and I don't like them, but I use them if God says to use.

Plow stands for poor, lost, orphaned widow. Come on, that's what the Bible says we're supposed to look out for, the body of Christ is supposed to look out for the poor, the lost, the orphaned or the widow, I don't know about you, but we can't take care of any of them if we're poor. Come on, if we can barely keep our finances of our own, OK, then guess what, we're not going to be taking care of anybody else. The body of Christ is supposed to be blessed to help bless the nation. Come on, there's not supposed to be I'm going to say this, there's not supposed to be ever bins in any time in our life. There was never supposed to be public aid. There was never supposed to be any help from food stamps or link card whatever to the modern-day term is. there is not supposed to be ever, why? Because the church was supposed to be the ones looking out for those. But see, the church got broke because guess what, they can't handle the rebellion. Well, you know it or not, rebellions be going on for a long, long time. You say, oh, I don't believe. Let's just think about the 70s. Come on. People driving around in minivans, smoking marijuana, protesting wars who don't have a job. I love when they protest, and they don't even they've never had a job. Some have never graduated high school and they're protesting I don't understand the 70s. I thank God I was born when I was born in the 70s. So, you got to understand. So, I got to miss some of that because I was too little to understand. But I'm telling you, we get into a place to where we don't even realize that was a rebellious generation. Some of us come from a rebellious generation, but let me tell you something, we're living in a day right now. It's nothing compared to what's coming. This is just a little nip nugget in the middle of this that we needed to hear, because how many know the harvest is about to come. And when it comes, we think of people coming in here who want to be here. Now they're going to come here because somebody's got them here, somebody convinced them to come to a service. And they're not going to like it. They're not going to like it one bit, especially when God starts dealing with issues.

Come on, we have religion who's come here, and they didn't like it when God dealt with their issues, even though they wanted deliverance, they wanted one on one deliverance. Well, God was trying to do it in a deeper way, and they still are bucking against it. I believe they probably will come back, but that's beside the point. After they get over their pity party, they'll be back. How many times can we get upset? Why? Because we're still a rebellious people. We can get upset about anything, to and for what we just get upset so fast. Good thing you brought your shield. That was a knee slapper wasn't it, let's move on. I don't know if I've had a point tonight, but this is a point right here, storms and confusion stir, but God reigns above it all. Storms and confusion stir, but God reigns above it all. That's why I keep saying we should already we have been through this enough. We should know he's got us. He's got it, it doesn't matter how bad anything gets and it doesn't matter what how delayed it looks, he is in charge. We have been in and seen many storms as of late, but in the midst of this, God has us in his hand. In the midst of this, I saw what appeared like four living creatures in Revelations. And this was their appearance, which a lot of this can be confirmed in scripture, but I got this straight from the throne of God first one of these days, I made use of drawing of this. Each one now, those are the details you want to get in there listening to these details. Poor living creatures. This was their appearance. They had a human form. Each one of them had four faces and four wings and their legs were straight, and the soles of their feet were like calf's hoof. They sparkled and gleamed like shiny bronze under their wings on their four sides they had human hands. And we wonder why people skip over this. And as for the faces and wings of the four of them, their wings touched one another. Their faces did not turn when they moved. Each went straightforward. want you to hear that. When they moved. The head did not turn in each of the four faces went straight.

It's impossible in the natural. Regarding the form and appearance of their faces, they each had the face of a man in front. And each had the face of a lion on the right side. And the face of an ox on the left side and all four also had the face of an eagle at the back of their heads. Such as were their faces. Their wings were stretched out upward, two wings of each one was touching another, the wings of the beings, because that's what they are, beings. On either side of it and the remaining two wings of each being were covered and covering their bodies. And each went straightforward and wherever the spirit was about to go, they would go without turning as they went. Among the living beings there was something they looked like burning poles of fire, like torches moving back and forth among living beings, and the fire was bright, and lightning was flashing and from the fire and the living beings move rapidly back and forth like flashes of lightning. Now, as I look at the beings, I saw one wheel on the ground. Is anybody in there yet? Hallelujah, hallelujah. One wheel on the ground beside the living beings for each of the four of them regarding the appearance of the wheels. Remember, revelations have wheel within a wheel. It refers to the wheel. I'm getting into that now. And their construction, they gleamed like beryl, olivine. Chrysolite, I think, is what it's called, and the four were made alike and their appearance and construction were a real. Set out the right angle within a wheel. So, you got to understand the wheel was actually made up of creatures. And when they moved, they went in any one of their four directions, so all of a sudden, the wheels started turning and they went that way. And when the wheels started turning, they went whichever head face. We take them. And regarding their rims because wheels have rims, right, they were so high. That they were awesome and dreadful and the rims of all four of them were full of eyes all around scripture refers to eyes were all around the wheels. So, these wheels turn. There's eyes all around them. Whenever the living beings move, the wheels move with them. And when the living beings rose from the earth, the wheels rose also, and wherever the spirit went, the beings went in that direction and the wheels rose along with them for the spirit or life of the living beings was in the wheels. Whenever those went, these went and whenever those came to a stop, these came to a stop and when those rose from the earth, the wheels roll close behind them for the spirit of the living beings was in the wheels.

Now, a lot of this and some of this, especially as in Ezekiel two chapter one, verse four through twenty-eight, I'm not going to spend a lot of time there because I have a lot I want to still get into. But Ezekiel, chapter one, verse four through twenty-eight, you're going to see a lot of vision of what God just talked about. And I believe some of this man, we can never wrap our brain around it, just looking at it. That's why I say there's got to come a day when I need to get this on paper. We need to actually see exactly what God saying. This is what happens. And, man, because it's so much little detail revelations, Ezekiel, Daniel, have so much detail at the end of the world. We have to have it now. We cannot wait until we're in the midst of the Antichrist battling and everything else and start trying to get revelation. We need to have the revelation before that. How many knows. So, we're going to get into some of that. But Ezekiel chapter one, verse four through twenty-eight has a lot. The four living creatures' appearances include faces of a man, a lion, an ox, and an eagle. There is a strong, prophetic symbolism of these images, how many know there's a prophetic thing spoken about each one of these? The face of a man represents humankind. We are workers, do you know where workers of the field helping the tent bring harvest the face of a lion represents Christ. The lion of Judah, who breaks the chains of every demonic curse on every assignment. That's why we need this right now. We need this part of it. This revelation, if we can comprehend and get it in our spirit, we will actually break everything, every time, everywhere we go. Because we will not be dealing with anything the same that we've dealt with it in the past, and it'll be just like the wheel within the wheel, just like the living creatures, when they move, the wheel moves, and everything moves together and then you start taking care of one another. Things start tearing down, things start breaking down. I'm telling you, the faces of the ox. Let's get into some more detail about this. The face of the ox serves as a reminder of Breakthru, and ox pulls the plow to break up. Come on, it breaks up the ground for harvest. He's caring for the plow, the poor, the lost, the orphan and the widow. I love this one.

The eagle represents divine perspective and vision. The Eagles can see and as the eagle soars flying higher and higher, he brings clarity and vision to the seer in the prophets. I want you to think about something. Some of the visions I released in the belly of revival was talking about Eagles. I believe God was trying to tap me into this type of thing, and I got so far into it. But some were stopped. And those visions, I believe, were in the back of one of the books of breakthrough of spiritual strongholds I believe it is, but those visions, I believe, are for such a time as this. And just like the soil being turned for harvest fields, the upheaval right now in the world means that nations and continents are under great attack. It's gotten so crazy right now that people are trying to blame Trump for what's going on in France. What's going on in Europe? It's a most chaotic nonsense I've never seen in my life. That's why the four living creatures are about to be turned like never before, and some of the manifestations of that prophetic fulfillment of what they are meant to be. Seraphim and angels are being released, which seraphim are types of angels being released on our behalf to do minister to us and to help us and get us ready and to cleanse us when we need cleansing to take us deeper. That's all about to happen in such a realm that we're about to get a little crazy up in here. Here's what I hope my microphone works, but this what I saw the spirit. Movement is going to come a movement. It's going to happen so much that sometimes angels are going to be coming in and going out, coming in and going out, moving, going about, stirring, dropping things, doing things. And then religion is going to walk in, and some people are even going to get to their seat. But don't be spooked to leave. Because it's religion. This kind of stuff is not going to fit in religion. Come on. If I preach this tonight and. More than half of the people that's been coming here in the last few months, they'd already back, their head wouldn't probably spin it because it's unchartered territory. There's a lot of people will not touch this stuff. We sing songs with details of it, but we will not ever comprehend it unless we dig into it.

Sometimes you don't know you like spinach till you start dishing it up. Sometimes you don't know if you like something till you start trying. But people are going to come in and they're going to they're going to plug right in and they're going to be people is going to just be rejecting it just by what they feel. You know what? And we cannot take that personally. We've had people walk out of our services before they walk in and look at the tape table and they leave. I just pray they look at the book table. That should tell a story right there. Come on. You know, break through and overcoming the power of lust and, you know, destroying the Jezebel spirit. There's a few things out there can mess a person up. See, the storms are becoming more fervent, and the enemy is on the rampage to destroy our faith. That's why more than ever before, he wants to destroy our faith. But we're supposed to be of a different level, things that bother us are not supposed to be bothering us. And the word in Ezekiel reminds us that God is a ruler. He is the ruler and judge and I'm talking about the courts of heaven; he reigns over the courtroom of heaven and the enemy is the prosecutor. Many people, especially I don't like to refer to this, but we have to, in the Western culture, can't wrap their minds around the supernatural. The church is dumb when it comes to supernatural. I remember years ago when I was 11, I was in the Litchfield revival. We'd already had meetings scheduled when Litchfield revival broke out, so I had to go to Springfield, Illinois, in the midst of revival. So, when I'd been in Springfield over and over and over again, God moved, he healed, he set free. But I never tapped into the presence of God before. So, this time in the midst of the Litchfield revival, I was talking about the glory, and I can hear in the spirit many people were murmuring during the teaching. What's the glory? What is it? Why does he keep saying glory? What's that mean? And it was one of the deader services. Because people cannot wrap their mind around this stuff. Especially the stuff I've referred to tonight. Four faced creatures and this is not somebody you want to eat dinner with unless you know. If you see a wheel spinning around, has eyes all around it. But the word says a cloud with fire flashing continually from it and brightness was around it, and in its core, there was something like glowing amber colored metal in the midst of the fire. And within that, they were figures resembling the four living beings.

You know, Ezekiel goes on to describe in great detail of what was revealed to him, what he saw, and it was nothing short of supernatural. Ezekiel was constantly in the supernatural. I wrote a book on the supernatural, and that was super. Come on. But I believe the supernatural that I believe I'm talking about right now makes that book look like Sunday school. Come on, glory, signs and wonders, presence of God, great stuff, but I'm talking about we're about to tap into a quart of heaven. That's going to look like some of the greatest sci fi movies we've ever seen. Some of the things your superheroes and things you've seen on some of those shows and different things are actually created from someone who's read the word of God, and they took some of those details and put it into the television and people are excited about it. And whether you know it or not, there were superheroes in heaven long before any of these people. And the only difference is heaven is real. Did I just ruin it for you? You thought Supergirl was real, didn't you? Let's move on.

See, supernatural activity is all around us, and the sooner you can acknowledge it and embrace it, the sooner we will be able to understand how God speaks. His mysteries come through the supernatural. Come on, no matter how you receive a prophetic word, it's supernatural, whether the voice comes from heaven and goes through you, or someone drops down and whispers to you, it doesn't matter what level, it's supernatural. Every sermon I prepare, every person I prophecies to, everything I see, it's supernatural. If just haven't had enough let's have a little more. One of the things I kept seeing is chariots, God took me to Zechariah, Chapter six. Four chariots, four chariots. Hallelujah. Starting verse one, chapter six. Now, again, I looked up and the four chariots were coming out from between the two mountains and the mountains were mountains of bronze and then the word of God bronze. I looked up the word bronze means divine judgment. The chariots are released in the midst of divine judgment. This is some of the stuff I want to just brush on really quick, we're not we're not in it yet, but here it comes. The first chariot had red horses, red horses stood for war, bloodshed. The second, the second chariot had black horses. Black stood for the famine and death. The third chariot had white horses; the white horses stood for victory. And the four chariot has strong dappled horses. Which stood for death through judgment.

Then I said to the angel who was speaking with me, what are these my Lord, the angel answered, these are the four spirits of heaven. Which go out after presenting themselves before the Lord of all the Earth, with the chariot, with the black horses going toward the north country and then the one with the white horses follows them behind. Because there are two northern powers to overcome. And the chariot with the devil horses goes toward the south country. And when the strong horses went out, they were eager to patrol the Earth and the Lord said, go patrol the Earth, and so they patrolled the earth, watching and protecting it. And then he called out to me and said to me, see, those who are going to north country have quieted my spirit of wrath, to the north country. I know you all heard this last time you were at Sunday school. Let's look at some of this and think about some of this. I see Chariots of Fire. They rode in swiftly across the sky. That's what I saw by the spirit Chariots of Fire. We've all read some of the scripture. You know. Angels were setting on Chariots of Fire that came to rescue. I want you to think about something. I saw his divine glory, God's divine glory, shattered thrones of the Second Heaven. There's many thrones in the second heaven. Shattering the thrones, I knew immediately that God was saying that he is dismantling demonic assignments that have held you back. If it's held you back, I want you to get this, I got the anointing all over me right now. I don't care if you get it right now. This is on me. Every time something, I hold you back long enough, a throne gets created in that heaven. Why? Because that. Second heaven has declared dominion over your life. Thrones get created in second heaven because they have dominion. And these Chariots of Fire get released to break the Dominion. In the word of God, I just read it, talked about the wrath was about to be released, but these angels of these chariots were released to do some cleaning up. And because of what they did, because of how successful they did it, God's wrath was removed.

I want you to think about some of these things, because here's what God said, God said, he's dismantling the demonic assignments that have held you back. Destiny is now upon us. It is time to align ourselves to God's plan, come on and just to displace and dismantle the reigning powers of darkness over specific regions. I don't know about you, but the enemy is not going to reign over my house or our house and any more of the details that he's been raining, come on, guys. Wanted to take us to another dimension. We don't have to stay here. delay doesn't mean dominion. If we have a delay in something, it doesn't mean the enemy has dominion. But see when we get so caught up in the delay. And get bound by the delay that gives him the dominion. I'll spend a little more time on this than what I planned, but I'm here and we need this because we're breaking the backbone of the enemy and he's going to have some thrones busted. I don't know about you, but I like picture I like to picture the thrones in second heaven like porcelain, you know, they shatter. Come on, you ever try to take a toilet out? If you can't get it out, just shatter that thing and shatter, fine. I've shattered them when I didn't want to shatter them. So that's beside the point. So, we must take ownership of our callings and run come on with perseverance to fulfill the destinies. All right, I'll say this. Millions are waiting on us. Because when you begin to break the Dominion, you're not just breaking for you, you're breaking it for every person that gets bound by the same throne, dominion means it's a place of domination. It's a place of authority. It's a place of legal right. And every time we break something, it breaks the power or the contract or the agreement for any person who is under that law, under that authority. So, when you break that dominion over a region or over a nation over something, it breaks off of every person it's associated with. Millions are waiting on us. You can do it any time because I got it. Now, see, they're waiting for hope. People are waiting. They're waiting for hope. They don't know how to find this. Nobody's teaching. Nobody's telling them how to get to it. They cannot understand the word of God or have enough in their DNA at this time because they barely can live, they barely can get by. They can barely get through their addictions. And the dominion has to be broke by somebody. We're laying the groundwork so people can work with it, Wigglesworth and people like Katherine Kuhlman did it, people like John G Lake did it, even people like Moses and oh and Joshua. I'm telling you, all across the world there are people who have done it, churches, little churches have done it. And I'm telling you, we are right now getting ready to break open some things for millions of people. It doesn't matter how few we have; we're breaking something for millions.

That's why God wants to bless us, the level he wants to bless us. Because it's a reward, it's like heaven is going to open over you. See, here's what God says, I'm establishing borders in the natural and in the spirit realm, I'm removing and destroying the land markers that the enemy laid to keep you behind boundary lines. Say God never intended for you to be limited by boundaries. So, when you break a throne here, you're not limited to break the throne just here, you can break it in South Africa, you can break that throne wherever it is you break it internationally. We're not bound by those lines. So, is it time to step over these boundaries? Come on, redeem our inheritances, anybody here got inheritances, been spoken for your property, for your family, for your children, for your finances, for your health. Come on. If cancer can say goodbye, I don't care what the devil says. We are in a time if God can heal cancer or stop cancer in his tracks, he can break open the financial realm. The throne's try to create in our life every time we start to focus on it, we start to dwell on it, we start to get caught up in it. A week goes by and we're still moaning and groaning. A throne is starting to be constructed. Why, because it's dominating, it's having dominion. It's our life now, it's our focus now. So, when you begin to cut it off and release it to God and you start tapping into the four living creatures that come on the Chariots of Fire, the Seraphim Angels, and you're tapping into an unknown power that you've never known before.

See I want you to understand, one time God told me and some of you are going to be like, Yeah, says in a word, he's coming back for a glorious church. I'm like, Yeah, here's what I said to God one time. I said, I don't know how you're going to do it. I can never I can never imagine the church being glorious. Come on, it's a wimpy, wimpy church. Come on. Very few across America. I mean, we got to drive hours, an hour somewhere to get something, it's ridiculous. So, I was just being real about anybody ever be real with God? I'm just being real with him. And I'm like, I don't see this ever happening. You're coming back for your church. That must not have the broad understanding of glorious you know; it must be glorious for a minute. And here's what he said. And I want you to understand, I did not know what he said, but I heard what he said. When all of heaven connects with the church. Heaven will make the church glorious. See the chariots went this way and went that way and went this way as orders by God. Nowhere in the scriptures before and after those referred to because a man of God did something big for this to happen. This was just heaven invading Earth. I want you to understand, there's things that we have experienced here on Earth that we don't even realize we're heaven ordained miracles. See sometimes people on December twenty fourth are looking in the sky hoping for a glimpse of Santa Claus. One of these days, they're going to look up and see a real chariot of fire. They're going to think they got Santa Claus going by, but instead of saying, ho, ho, ho, it's going to be saying glory to the Lord of all the Earth. Because I'm telling you something, there's a move that takes place in heaven that can line up the church like that. You want to get some churches, right? Imagine if a chariot landed right on Sunday morning. Those that don't run out screaming and hollering, God will take you into a new dimension. I believe he's got the glorious church, no problem. But in my mind, I thought, there's no way.

This church, the church is pathetic, I mean, my goodness, nobody's praying, nobody knew about 9/11 hardly. And they all said they knew after the fact, but nobody knew before. All kinds of myths, prophetic words, and this and that and alignment's and this and falling and rising, and we're supposed to collab with heaven, not trying to do it ourselves. There's too many conferences and church services and apostolic services and prophetic services and this and that. Whatever you just start tapping into open heavens supernatural, doing exactly what God wants to do. Let the angels come down and do the hard handling and do the anointing touch. And whatever happens, happens. And you'll be like, well, somebody touched me. Who was it? Was it the men of God? Or was it the woman of God. It was just somebody touched me. See all that has been taken from you, stolen from you all is going to return to you seven-fold, because when he breaks the Dominion, the thrones. The contract says severalfold. See second heaven has dominion right now in some areas of our life and the areas of the United States, but when those dominions are broke, that contract also says that when these are broke, when these are severed, when these are destroyed, seven-fold return, when these are broke, when these are severed, and these are destroyed. Seven-fold return. Come on. And we'll try to say this, I hope you can catch it. I didn't double check this one hundred percent, this part, so bear with me, but this is what I believe. Usually I confirm things, but I forgot to confirm this one. So, some I'll say it like I know what I'm talking about. I believe I do, but I never checked it. Hallelujah. Hallelujah. Come on. I fact check myself. You have to fact check. And what I mean by that is because God said this is the year of five seven. It's the year of the sickle and the sword. But the sevens represent spiritual perfection, completion.

God is releasing his kingdom and his laws are set in place, say you're going to see restoration in your family, all losses will cease in the name of Jesus. God is releasing governmental rods. This is when the rest of the crowd would have kicked in. They wouldn't have got here till now. They just showed up in the spirit. And God is releasing governmental rods of new authority to the apostles, prophets and pastors that will bring alignment in the House of God. Get ready. A shaking is going on. And it and is by his design and his hand, he comes as a mighty rushing wind, by the way. That's my title. Unstoppable, unstoppable, no matter what resistance or stronghold attempts to stand against him, let's allow the rushing wins, the Holy Spirit to rush over us and reset our traps. Perfectly positioning us to where we are called to be in the next season. There are breaker anointing that will be released upon my people as they operate in the supernatural realms. These Braker anointings will be Catullus to the full turnaround in their lives, a turning away from limitations. The songs were so perfect tonight and hindrances and into places of freedom and fullness of life. And the next season may our emphasis be to boldly follow the winds of the spirit, serve the least of these and stand firm as he restores everything sevenfold, just as he has promised. Again, I say to you, the title tonight is like a mighty rushing wind. God is coming in. To shake things up. Some of it, is it going to be what you've done, it's not going because you prayed all night long, because you fasted, it's not good because you have anointing oil. It's going to because God's drawn the line in the sand and he's releasing chariots. Come on. We read in the scripture. Where secrets were being revealed and we read where, you know, the servant comes out and says, man, they are going to come and kill us. I believe it was Elijah. I'm just going off the top of my head. Prayed for the eyes of a servant to be opened and his servant was able to see angels. Setting out Chariots of Fire. This was because this was a man of God doing exactly what he was supposed to do. And that's it.

Sometimes we're doing what we're supposed to do and the enemy's coming for us. But if we know that, we know. He can release angelic breaking. Breaker anointing was supernatural right in our midst, the right angels can be going this way, the right angels can go this way, and that can cause total release just by them being in the realm of the spirit. And I saw angels just flying across the sky. Just flying across the sky on Chariots of Fire. So, imagine for a moment if you're in the midst of a battle and Chariots of Fire shows up, if you're in the midst of something that you're believing for and just one living creature shows up, they all four shows up, they got faces on all sides of their face, head one over here, one over there, one back here, one here. And their face never turns. They just go the direction wherever they got to go. And they got a wheel turning with eyes on it. So where does our help come from. Our help actually comes from the supernatural. It's no wonder the church has been so beaten down because we're not accepting this type of realm. But I don't know about you, but it's time for us to accept it all. It's time for us to tap into some of this stuff. Come on and read about the wheel within the wheel, the four living creatures. Read about some of the details. Why just give get the spirit. This is what kind of thing God's about to do. And when you get tired, imagine for a minute that God can send an angel or a certain level of an angel called a seraphim will come to you and he can just wipe your lips with a fiery, hot, cold, fresh out of the altar. But it won't burn you. Think about some of this. Some of you would be flipped out if you saw any of this. Sometimes when you're transported in spirit, we've been transported, I believe Chariots of Fire has something to do with it.

Come on. I told the story many times years ago of where I was driving down the road and our car was bald tires, and it felt like the car got lifted up into the air. And by the time we got to the next city, all four tires were brand new needles still on the tires. I believe something changed them on the way there. And I and I don't think it was a mistake that the tire brand was master craft. Come on, it could have been any type of, you know, awesome brand, but it was master craft. Why, because I believe the master took care of it. We're in this. We're in this. And we didn't just accept the supernatural. Accept it, and if you don't understand it, don't reject it. To say I receive it anyway. I receive it anyway, the end of the world is coming, folks, and we need to tap into the supernatural now or we're not going to know what happens. I don't think it's a mistake, only several people over the years have really tapped into this type of realm that God wanted to take us to. Because it's unchartered territory. You can't read a lot on it, you can't ask, you know, so-and-so, pastor so-and-so, you can't just go down to a church and say, hey man, have you seen the Chariots of Fire? They'll be like, what is that? A band? You know. You know, is that one of those new bands out there. How about the four living creatures? Have you ever seen the eagle head, its amazing man? By that time, he has an appointment. Come on here, something has to do now. He needs to mow the yard, get home to kids, something now he's already disconnected his conversation. I'm telling you; the round guy wants to take us to all we have is the word of God in our faith. Come on. Because you can't trust every book that's out there that talks about it because they'll take you in 10 different directions. We have to have exactly what God wants to say.

Let the winds come right now in Jesus's name. Last, my wife will play a song. While the song plays, I want you understand, heaven right now is collecting our numbers. What I mean by that, God knows your number. He knows exactly where you live. He knows exactly what you're going to do, what you've done, and he's going to actually begin to call some of the supernatural to begin to invade your world. And what it's time to for the thrones to be broken in heaven, second heaven. Because it's time for the dominion to stop, some of us have been battling against the dominion in our finances, we get a breakthrough all the way up to a point, and it won't ever go past because of that dominion. The dominion is stopping tonight. So, it's time to get back pay. Come on, miss payments. See what happens sometimes with an if somebody is not paying child support and they don't do it for a long period of time and they end up getting taxes, most of the time, the government will just invade their taxes and take it and give it to the person that was supposed to get it in the first place. Well, some of us don't even realize the wealth of the wicked is about to be laid out for the righteous in such a way, and people, religion don't like what I say it like that. Wealth of the wicked going to be laid up for the righteous because I say it's supposed to already be laid up for the righteous. But the reason I say it, the way God just said it is because I believe there's drug dealers, criminals, mafia, the mob. Illegal politicians. You know, protesting type of governments that have robbed and stolen so long that God's going to tap into some of those hidden vaults. Come on. I know, but I don't believe they found all of Osama bin Laden's money. I don't believe they found all of Saddam Hussein's money. Come on. I don't know about you, but there's things that's going to be found and the enemy, it doesn't matter how they look over time that you might have something appear into your hands. It's going to be of an international money. You'd be like, how'd that get here, angelic help. There are things about to get crazy. But we need it because everything that we know now, there will come a day where we're not going to be able to know it. There will come a day. You're not going to be able to tap into your cell phone. You're not going to be able to use TomTom or some kind of you know service to find your way anywhere, there's not going to be a Wi-Fi or anything, you're not gonna be able to connect to the Internet, you're not going be able to have a cell phone because we're going to have to have supernatural. Just so you know, heaven has better games than the phone. Hallelujah. Let's worship for a little bit and let God go through and take care of some business.

## Don't miss out!

Visit the website below and you can sign up to receive emails whenever Bill Vincent publishes a new book. There's no charge and no obligation.

https://books2read.com/r/B-A-XHBC-UCHRB

BOOKS 2 READ

Connecting independent readers to independent writers.

# Also by Bill Vincent

Building a Prototype Church: Divine Strategies Released
Experience God's Love: By Revival Waves of Glory School of the Supernatural
Glory: Expanding God's Presence
Glory: Increasing God's Presence
Glory: Kingdom Presence of God
Glory: Pursuing God's Presence
Glory: Revival Presence of God
Rapture Revelations: Jesus Is Coming
The Prototype Church: Heaven's Strategies for Today's Church
The Secret Place of God's Power
Transitioning Into a Prototype Church: New Church Arising
Spiritual Warfare Made Simple
Aligning With God's Promises
A Closer Relationship With God
Armed for Battle: Spiritual Warfare Battle Commands
Breakthrough of Spiritual Strongholds
Desperate for God's Presence: Understanding Supernatural Atmospheres
Destroying the Jezebel Spirit: How to Overcome the Spirit Before It Destroys You!
Discerning Your Call of God
Glory: Expanding God's Presence: Discover How to Manifest God's Glory

Glory: Kingdom Presence Of God: Secrets to Becoming Ambassadors of Christ
Satan's Open Doors: Access Denied
Spiritual Warfare: The Complete Collection
The War for Spiritual Battles: Identify Satan's Strategies
Understanding Heaven's Court System: Explosive Life Changing Secrets
A Godly Shaking: Don't Create Waves
Faith: A Connection of God's Power
Global Warning: Prophetic Details Revealed
Overcoming Obstacles
Spiritual Leadership: Kingdom Foundation Principles
Glory: Revival Presence of God: Discover How to Release Revival Glory
Increasing Your Prophetic Gift: Developing a Pure Prophetic Flow
Millions of Churches: Why Is the World Going to Hell?
The Supernatural Realm: Discover Heaven's Secrets
The Unsearchable Riches of Christ: Chosen to be Sons of God
Deep Hunger: God Will Change Your Appetite Toward Him
Defeating the Demonic Realm
Glory: Increasing God's Presence: Discover New Waves of God's Glory
Growing In the Prophetic: Developing a Prophetic Voice
Healing After Divorce: Grace, Mercy and Remarriage
Love is Waiting
Awakening of Miracles: Personal Testimonies of God's Healing Power
Deception and Consequences Revealed: You Shall Know the Truth and the Truth Shall Set You Free
Overcoming the Power of Lust
Cover Up and Save Yourself: Revealing Sexy is Not Sexy
Heaven's Court System: Bringing Justice for All
The Angry Fighter's Story: Harness the Fire Within
The Wrestler: The Pursuit of a Dream
Beginning the Courts of Heaven: Understanding the Basics

Breaking Curses: Legal Rights in the Courts of Heaven
Writing and Publishing a Book: Secrets of a Christian Author
How to Write a Book: Step by Step Guide
The Anointing: Fresh Oil of God's Presence
Spiritual Leadership: Kingdom Foundation Principles Second Edition
The Courts of Heaven: How to Present Your Case
The Jezebel Spirit: Tactics of Jezebel's Control
Heaven's Angels: The Nature and Ranking of Angels
Don't Know What to Do?: Discover Promotion in the Wilderness
Word of the Lord: Prophetic Word for 2020
The Coronavirus Prophecy
Increase Your Anointing: Discover the Supernatural
Apostolic Breakthrough: Birthing God's Purposes
The Healing Power of God: Releasing the Power of the Holy Spirit
The Secret Place of God's Power: Revelations of God's Word
The Rapture: Details of the Second Coming of Christ
Increase of Revelation and Restoration: Reveal, Recover & Restore
Leadership vs Management
Restoration of the Soul: The Presence of God Changes Everything
Building a Prototype Church: The Church is in a Season of Profound of Change
Keys to Receiving Your Miracle: Miracles Happen Today
The Resurrection Power of God: Great Exploits of God
Transitioning to the Prototype Church: The Church is in a Season of Profound of Transition
Waves of Revival: Expect the Unexpected
The Stronghold of Jezebel: A True Story of a Man's Journey
Glory: Pursuing God's Presence: Revealing Secrets
Like a Mighty Rushing Wind
Steps to Revival

Watch for more at https://revivalwavesofgloryministries.com/.

## About the Author

Bill Vincent is no stranger to understanding the power of God. Not only has he spent over twenty years as a Minister with a strong prophetic anointing, he is now also an Apostle and Author with Revival Waves of Glory Ministries in Litchfield, IL. Along with his wife, Tabitha, he, leads a team providing apostolic oversight in all aspects of ministry, including service, personal ministry and Godly character.

Bill offers a wide range of writings and teachings from deliverance, to experiencing presence of God and developing Apostolic cutting edge Church structure. Drawing on the power of the Holy Spirit through years of experience in Revival, Spiritual Sensitivity, and deliverance ministry, Bill now focuses mainly on pursuing the Presence of God and breaking the power of the devil off of people's lives.

His books 50 and counting has since helped many people to overcome the spirits and curses of Satan. For more information or to keep up with Bill's latest releases, please visit www.revivalwavesofgloryministries.com. To contact Bill, feel free to follow him on twitter @revivalwaves.

Read more at https://revivalwavesofgloryministries.com/.

# About the Publisher

Accepting manuscripts in the most categories. We love to help people get their words available to the world.

Revival Waves of Glory focus is to provide more options to be published. We do traditional paperbacks, hardcovers, audio books and ebooks all over the world. A traditional royalty-based publisher that offers self-publishing options, Revival Waves provides a very author friendly and transparent publishing process, with President Bill Vincent involved in the full process of your book. Send us your manuscript and we will contact you as soon as possible.

Contact: Bill Vincent at rwgpublishing@yahoo.com www.rwgpublishing.com

www.ingramcontent.com/pod-product-compliance
Lightning Source LLC
LaVergne TN
LVHW042004060526
838200LV00041B/1874